THE CHURCH AT WAR

THE CHURCH AT

RECLAIMING THE DYSFUNCTIONAL CHURCH

WAR

GOD'S ASSASSIN

RONALD FRAKER

Pleasant Word (a division of WinePress Publishing, PO Box 428, Enumclaw, WA 98022) functions only as book publisher. As such, the ultimate design, content, editorial accuracy, and views expressed or implied in this work are those of the author.

Unless otherwise noted, all Scriptures are taken from the *Holy Bible, New International Version®*, NIV®. Copyright © 1973, 1978, 1984 by the International Bible Society. Used by permission of Zondervan. All rights reserved.

Scripture references marked KJV are taken from the *King James Version* of the Bible.

Scripture references marked NASB are taken from the *New American Standard Bible,* © 1960, 1963, 1968, 1971, 1972, 1973, 1975, 1977 by The Lockman Foundation. Used by permission.

ISBN 13: 978-1-4141-1344-9
ISBN 10: 1-4141-1344-7
Library of Congress Catalog Card Number: 2009902469

CONTENTS

THE ASSASSIN

LET ME TELL you about a miracle that took place one Sunday morning when a stranger walked into church. The church had already lost three pastors in five years. Now the rumor was that another pastor was leaving. People quietly whispered that the reason these pastors left was that none of them could submit to Brother John, a founding member of the church. Brother John was also the president of the board and the main financial supporter. It was often said that without Brother John, the church would die.

This particular Sunday morning started the same as always. The members were scattered throughout the sanctuary. The choir was slowly making its way to the front of the church. Organ music filled the room when the back doors opened and a stranger slowly walked in.

He looked around and then took a seat with his back against the wall. From this vantage point, he could see everything that took place. He sat quietly through the service, involved but still detached. Afterward, the stranger somberly greeted the pastor. In a strong, quiet voice he said, "Today is the day!"

After his customary five minutes of greeting people, Brother John left the church and walked to his car in its reserved parking spot. As he opened the door, the stranger approached him. He engaged Brother John in conversation. No one heard what they said, but their body language spoke loud and clear.

Brother John's face turned red. He raised his voice, but the stranger just looked at him with cold, piercing eyes. Then the most unusual thing happened. Brother John's knees began to shake, his breath came in gasps, and his shoulders trembled uncontrollably. He collapsed into the driver's seat of his car. After a few minutes needed to regain his composure, he drove from the church parking lot, never to be seen again. The stranger looked across the lot at the pastor, tipped his head, and quietly left the area.

Five years after that fateful Sunday morning, that same pastor and his family are still leading the church. A new joy and a renewed faith have swept over the congregation. The day the stranger came into the church was the day the bondage over it was broken. Now many members, both old and new, can enjoy God's anointing as they continue to grow together.

The above story is fictional, but I believe there are a few churches that could use the services of the "stranger." The stranger was there to rid the church of the stranglehold Brother John had on the congregation. This kind of control destroys good pastors and weakens the anointing of a church.

The stranger was not a pastor, but I am sure the pastor came to appreciate his ministry. The ministerial position the stranger fulfilled could only be described as an "assassin."

Assassin Needed

This book presents the theory that the office of the assassin existed in the Old Testament as well as in the New Testament. There are scattered numerous examples of assassinations throughout the historical books of the Old Testament. The evidence surrounding the assassinations needs to be examined, and the personality of the assassin understood to fully appreciate the thesis of this book.

For the purpose of this book, an "assassination" is one person intentionally eliminating another person to benefit the overall health of an organizational entity. To put it in simpler terms, it's similar to eliminating termites from a wooden foundation so the structure might become stronger.

Termites slowly eat away the strength of a foundation until it eventually implodes. Many times, we never actually see the termites; we only see the evidence of their destruction. The damage is so gradual we often ignore their presence until the structure becomes unstable. It's only when the structure begins to fall that we become concerned about the termites. By that time, it is often too late to save the structure.

The assassin's job is to eliminate the termites before the structure is irreparably damaged. The Old Testament usage of the word *assassin* meant a literal taking of a human life. I am using *assassin* in a New Testament context best defined as a person who strongly encourages an entrenched insurgent who has burrowed deeply within the structure of a church to cease and desist his destructive actions and to release his stranglehold on the church. The assassin is equipped and trained to eradicate the gnawing termites from the wooden cross of Christ's churches.

There has never been a large demand for the assassin, but when you need one, it is comforting to know he exists. I would guess the reason there are so few assassins within the church world is because they make lousy party guests, but in the right situation, they are indispensable. I am writing about the "right situation," which is not the standard God-fearing church.

Every pastor or leader knows there are specific churches where someone needs to be intentionally removed so the church may be restored to its former glory. There are many churches where a person or a family has been able to establish a stronghold that tries to control the pastor, the members, and the anointing of the Holy Spirit. The anointing of the Holy Spirit breaks the yoke, so the anointing must be stifled for the stronghold to remain. The only way the stronghold is going to be removed is for the person to be either broken or removed.

We all know this action must take place, but we rarely talk about it publicly and even more rarely do we move to remedy the situation. If we do decide to take action, we are ill-prepared to do what's necessary and quite often we leave a large mess behind. We, as an army, are not trained or equipped to perform this maneuver.

The mistake we make is sending in sensitive and emotionally unprepared pastors and asking them to complete an assignment that requires an assassin's personality. This action requires a man to think and react like a soldier, not a longsuffering, emotionally sensitive shepherd. In the military, it would be like sending a chaplain to perform the job of a sniper. We need to send the right man to do the right job. We need an assassin to terminate the stronghold that is strangling the anointing of the church and injuring our pastors and their families.

So where is an assassin when you need him?

If I went to any established church and asked the senior pastor if I could talk to the church assassin, I would most likely be thrown out and asked not to return. Assassins do exist, but we choose to ignore them. We pretend they don't exist and hope we'll never need them. Assassins are hard to live with because of their unique personalities. They tend to be "different." These assassins do not do well as senior pastors of the standard God-fearing congregation, so they sit on the fringe of denominations waiting for the Special Forces to be called. They are often seen as "faithful," but rarely seen as "successful."

Since we do not recognize the need for an assassin, we have not defined how and where he should be used. Because we do not recognize the office of the assassin, we continue to send unprepared pastors into situations that will quickly overwhelm them. Out of frustration and desperation to solve a problem, they end up dropping a mega-bomb where a precision guided missile would have been more effective. The precision strike would have caused less collateral damage and the cleanup would have been easier.

As a result of fighting battles in the same manner that we always have, we end up with many pastors who suffer from Post Traumatic Stress Syndrome. Once a pastor has experienced the trauma of this particular battle, it will take years for him to recover from the emotional scars left by the encounter. If these pastors are not embraced, they will often commit positional suicide and leave the ministry. All of us know men and women who should still be in full-time ministry but are not. This statistic can and should be reversed.

Pastors belong to the "army of God." Biblically, we are described as being involved in warfare with a real enemy. As the battle rages, we are sending out kamikaze pilots who are sacrificed needlessly. If we really are an army involved in a battle, then we need to start thinking more like an army and less like a social club. Most of our churches are relatively at peace, but a few have been infiltrated and we need to take whatever action is necessary to reclaim God's land and rid those churches of the embedded insurgents.

THE ASSASSIN, BIBLICALLY SPEAKING

The main inspiration for the ministry of the assassin comes from the first two chapters of 1 Kings. David, the king of Israel, was well advanced in years and soon to relinquish his position as king. He had already promised the kingdom to his son, Solomon, but his other son, Adonijah, also wanted to be the king.

When Adonijah thought David was too weak to stop him, he gathered a group of like-minded insurgents who staged a coup and tried to take over the kingdom. This small group hosted a ceremony where they crowned Adonijah king.

Solomon's mother heard about this celebration and quickly informed David. She also reminded David of his promise concerning her son Solomon. David intervened and had the authorities anoint Solomon as king in a public ceremony. Solomon was then paraded through the city streets riding on King David's mule, therefore, officially making him king.

Once Adonijah and his group of insurgents realized they had lost the battle, they surrendered and begged for mercy. Solomon showed mercy to his brother but gave him the admonition that if he behaved in anything but an honorable manner, his life would be forfeited and he would be assassinated. Once David officially stepped down as king, he summoned Solomon to his bedside and gave him counsel regarding two other remaining problems.

A man named Shimei, a descendant of Saul, carried a deep hatred for David that culminated in Shimei chasing David while cursing and throwing stones at him. This occurred when Shimei thought David had been dethroned as king. Shimei was brave when he thought David was powerless, but he was a coward when he realized that David was still king. David should have had Shimei put to death for this act of treason, but for whatever reason, David let him live.

Next was Joab, the general of David's army. There was a long-standing problem between Joab and David that escalated to the point where Joab continually ignored David and did whatever he wanted.

All three of these men, Adonijah, Shimei, and Joab, had a total lack of respect for David as a man, but worse, they had no respect for the office of king. If they didn't respect the office when David held it, they would not respect the office when Solomon held it. They would always be a threat to the kingdom because of their lack of respect for the office, so Solomon was instructed to take care of the problem.

Concerning Shimei and Joab, Solomon was told not to let their grey hairs go to the grave without blood mixed in. In plain words, Solomon was told to have an assassin eliminate these problems. David instructed Solomon to take drastic action concerning a drastic situation.

THE ASSASSIN BENAIAH

Solomon understood the wisdom of David's instructions. He realized these problems were foundational and his kingdom could only be as strong as the foundation. Solomon knew the job of eliminating these three specific problems would require a man with unique talents and special abilities, so he searched for such a man. In Benaiah, Solomon found the exact combination of personality, physical ability, and specialized training that were required to complete this assignment.

Benaiah was a man of war and a general in the army. Having spent his life as a soldier, he was well trained and had the ability to eliminate problems quickly and efficiently. He would not waste time or effort as he fulfilled his assignment. This is important because "excessive time" allows for unseen problems to occur and easily complicate what should be a straightforward action. "Wasted effort" would indicate an incomplete plan or a lack of confidence or ability. Any of these situations would jeopardize the mission.

Benaiah was emotionally equipped to carry out this special assignment. He was emotionally able to take a man's life without hesitation and without undue personal trauma. Realizing there was a necessary job to do, he was able to accomplish that job with a detached indifference and logical approach that separated his emotions from his duty, thereby protecting him mentally.

A biblical example of the opposite personality is Peter. When the multitude came to the garden with clubs and swords to arrest Jesus, Peter found himself in the middle of a very emotional situation. The crowds had surrounded Jesus and were in the process of arresting the man whom Peter had served faithfully for three-and-a-half years. Peter, an emotional and spontaneous person by nature, now found himself facing the enemies of his Savior.

Adrenalin flowing, his emotions took over and without any logical basis, he whipped out his sword and cut off the ear of the servant of the high priest. This man was not even a leader or an instigator. He was not in a position of authority. He was simply a servant. Peter made such a mess of the situation that Jesus had to stop and put the man's ear back on.

I've always wondered why Peter cut the man's ear off. Losing one's ear is a minor inconvenience. There would be some pain and some loss of blood, but such a wound would not cause a man of war to hesitate. It wouldn't even slow him down. Peter's efforts on behalf of Jesus were a total waste of time and effort. Peter had no plan or logic. All he had was emotion and zeal.

If Peter had been an assassin, he would have carefully observed the situation from a position of advantage and logically formulated a plan. He would have been totally emotionless. He would have felt nothing but would have seen everything. He would have selected a target whose death would have created the most confusion, thereby allowing the opportunity for escape.

He would also have surveyed the terrain to locate the best place for an attack. It might have been in the midst of the crowd or it might have been on a deserted path, but the assassin would have chosen when and where the attack would take place. The assassin might even have decided an attack would be wasted effort at that time. He would not have stopped his efforts; he would only have postponed the attack until it could be effective. If the assassin did decide to attack, he would not merely cut off the poor man's ear, he would strike with deadly force and his thrust would reach its target.

In this example, I am not considering whether or not a defense of Jesus should have taken place. I am only using it to demonstrate the difference in the emotional makeup of various people.

Obviously, Solomon would not have hired a man like Peter to eliminate his three problems. Benaiah was the perfect man because he had a warrior's mentality and a winner's confidence that made him ideal for this assignment.

Benaiah also had to be something of a loner. He had to be willing to work alone and endure isolation to achieve the necessary victory. Most people work well with a group that offers support; the assassin is equipped to work alone under limited supervision. The supervisor assigns the mission and the assassin fulfills the mission.

Benaiah was the complete package and was ideally suited for this calling. Very few men are equipped with the complete array of tools necessary to be a successful assassin, but Benaiah was. Once Benaiah was given the assignment to eradicate these three insurgents, he set about the task in a very businesslike manner and quickly achieved success.

One key point to notice is that no innocent people were hurt. Benaiah surgically eliminated these three men and very few people were even aware that anyone had been assassinated. Benaiah moved quickly and efficiently and successfully fulfilled his mission.

Going back into the church world, I would suggest we often make the mistake of assigning a "Peter" to do the job of a "Benaiah" so we end up with many innocent people walking around with only one ear while the insurgents remain untouched.

THREE RULES TO BENAIAH'S SUCCESS

The key to Benaiah's success was that he used the following three rules in eliminating the problems.

Rule One: Be Straightforward

This rule presents a dichotomy of thought and reality. We all know the straightforward approach is the best method for dealing with a problem situation. The Bible clearly tells us that if we have a problem with a brother we are to go to him and confront him in a loving manner. We all know this, but we don't always obey.

What I see happening so often is that we skirt around the issue rather than dealing with the problem head on. We, including myself, often drop hints about a problem, hoping the perpetrator will guess what the problem is, rather than bringing it into the open. People don't have the ability to read minds, but everyone can read lips.

I learned this lesson firsthand many years ago when I was an evangelist. I had been away from home for an extended period of time and was looking forward to seeing my wife and children again. As I got off the plane, I saw my children, but I didn't recognize the woman holding their hands. When I left on this trip, my wife had shoulder length hair and this woman had very short hair. I was angry. I was so angry I don't think I even kissed her hello.

I decided to show my displeasure by giving her the silent treatment for at least a couple of days. The punishment I was giving didn't seem to have any effect. She didn't even ask why I wasn't talking to her. After a few days, I asked her if she wanted to know why I was giving her the silent treatment. She told me she hadn't noticed.

This surprised me, because I had done a really good job of not talking to her. I wondered how she could have missed the clear hints I had given? I felt that anyone should have recognized my excellent silent treatment. After I clearly explained the reasoning behind my actions and how she should look for these signs in the future, I realized I was in deep trouble. Now she was mad at my juvenile behavior and she did *not* give me the silent treatment. I learned a lesson that day and I am proud to say I have only made the same mistake a few times since then.

Many people, including pastors, shy away from confrontations. Most confrontations occur when one or the other person is forced into a corner and feels he or she has no other option. The problem with this method is that by the time we are cornered, emotions and hard feelings have entered the picture and a nasty situation usually emerges.

It is better to deal with the problem in a straightforward manner because there is a better chance of solving the situation quickly.

Rule Two: Be Logical

I have often found the first victim of confrontation is logic.

The Bible tells us to seek counsel. We are told there is wisdom in the counsel of friends. We all know this, so when we face a serious problem in our church we seek the counsel of our leaders or fellow pastors. We describe the problem and through rational, prayerful interaction, we detail the logical solution and how we should react to each step.

By the time we leave their counsel, we are comfortable with our detailed plan of action. We know exactly what to say and how to convey our thoughts in a spiritually uplifting manner. With peace in our hearts, we initiate the interaction with our nemesis, but it soon digresses into a confrontation. This is because we approach the problem with logic and the other party responds with emotions. Now we are in an out of control situation.

We started with a logical approach that fully made sense to our advisors and to us. Since our nemesis was not in on this plan, he responded with an emotional retort that was neither true nor logical. In reality, he took over the *interaction* and was now controlling the *confrontation*. Rule Two is to set a logical sequence of events that includes your response to a series of emotional distortions that can spiral out of control. When Shimei strayed from the logical sequence of events that had been detailed for him, Benaiah was quick to terminate him.

Here's an example of a situation that happened when I was the president of the council of a non-profit organization. I saw the council members and an employee operating in a manner that was neither legal nor ethical. I met with the organization's overseers and a logical sequence of events was detailed with the intention of restoring both the council and the employee. I convened a meeting with the council and the employee and logically approached the situation in the approved manner.

The meeting quickly digressed from a logical interaction to a full-blown emotional confrontation. After two hours, it became obvious that we were not going to reach an acceptable solution. Thankfully, the board and I had planned a response in case of such an occurrence. I took a letter out of my briefcase and read it to the council and the employee. It simply stated they were all terminated immediately, they should leave the premises within fifteen minutes, and anyone remaining would be arrested for trespassing.

Their response was instant shock followed by meek obedience. Logical preparation saved the day.

Rule Three: Be Quick

I must admit that following Rule Three is my biggest problem. Too many times I have let a situation continue that I know cannot have a happy ending. I keep hoping the situation will resolve itself, but it rarely does. In fact, the longer I let the situation drag on, the less chance it has of reaching a peaceful solution.

The longer a problem exists the less chance there is of reaching a humane conclusion. Once time and emotion enter the picture, someone is going to be severely hurt by the outcome and the scars will be visible for many years to come. The quicker the solution, the less chance anyone will be hurt.

Summary

There are so many lessons to be gleaned from Benaiah. These are the obvious ones:

Once Benaiah reached the conclusion that assassination was the only solution, he quit seeking other solutions and simply did what needed to be done. Talking was done and action was begun.

The Kingdom Is Now Established

After Benaiah completed his assignments, the Scripture states in 1 Kings 2:46:

> Thus the kingdom was established in the hand
> of Solomon.

Many of our churches exist but are not established in the hand of the pastor. We often pretend they are, but the truth is that someone else in the congregation holds the power. In some cases, we need to hire a Benaiah to eliminate the problems and to re-establish the church in the hand of the pastor.

SALVAGING OUR CHURCHES

SATAN, THE REAL ENEMY

THOUGH CHAPTER ONE dealt almost entirely with Solomon's reign, the purpose of this book is to examine how we might effectively salvage churches that have been infiltrated by insurgents and are under the control of the enemy. Ephesians 6:12 states:

> For we do not wrestle against flesh and blood, but against principalities, against powers, against the rulers of the darkness of this age, against spiritual hosts of wickedness in the heavenly places. (NKJV)

Our real enemy is Satan and his angels. The invisible battle is in the spiritual arena, but Satan uses humans to fulfill his agenda, so spiritual warfare often manifests in the physical realm.

The fact that the battle manifests in the flesh means we have casualties in the flesh as well. Some of those who bear the scars of battle are pastors who became victims of well-entrenched insurgents hidden deep within the fibers of our churches.

WOUNDED PASTORS

Many of these ministers are no longer involved in pastoral ministries because the enemy persuaded them they were failures when they could not meet the parameters of success generally accepted for churches. Healing and restoration can come to many of these pastors by showing them the truth behind their so-called failures.

I was attending a church health seminar when the instructor referred directly to the church I was then pastoring. He looked straight at me and said he didn't know how I had been able to survive in that church as long as I had. He had been the pastor of that same church for a couple of years and had left because he was not ready for the battle that was still raging. During those two years, he and his family had been severely wounded and years later still bore the scars of the conflict. His statement was clear evidence of the painful wounds inflicted during the battles and the continual healing still taking place.

This man was a veteran of many pastoral ministries. This pastor was not a novice. He had been in ministry for many years and had shepherded some very successful churches. He accepted the appointment to this troubled church believing it was ready for growth. He was a well-seasoned pastor with all the God-given tools necessary to lead a growing church.

Everyone, including the new pastor, expected the church to experience immediate growth because there was no visible reason to think otherwise. It was in an excellent location. The buildings were in very good condition and there was plenty of room to grow. You might assume this church was every pastor's dream, but it soon became a nightmare.

INSURGENTS AND SLEEPER CELLS

Insurgents were well hidden in this church. The spiritual walls seemed strong, but time would prove that spiritual termites were in the foundation. For two long years, this pastor tried to build the church, but all he experienced were landmines and snipers. It seemed that every place he walked, another explosion would occur. If he stood up, a sniper would try to terminate him.

A group of influential people portrayed themselves as the nucleus of the believers. They were vocal in their dissatisfaction, yet they refused to leave the church. Time would prove they were really a sleeper cell of insurgents trying to maintain control over their realm of influence. By all appearances, they were normal supporters, assisting wherever they could. In actuality, they were trying to destroy the foundation of the church and undermine whatever success the pastor might have.

Vulnerable Pastors

The pastor had a bigger problem than church growth; he had to worry about survival. He suffered many wounds because he did not have the assassin's personality. Because he did not recognize the true nature of that church, he was vulnerable to attack.

When I became pastor of the church, I didn't recognize its true nature either. I later became aware that the church was the Sodom and Gomorrah of the religious world. By that time, I had to patch up many cuts and wounds.

When I entered full-time ministry, I was retired from a local police department. I had worked the streets for four years and then served as a detective for six years. I thought I had seen every form of sin and degradation that exists in this world, but I was wrong.

It seemed as if every kind of vice known to man was well entrenched in this particular church. The insurgents protected the various vices from the meddling of the pastor and thought they were protecting the offenders from the Holy Spirit. If the pastor crossed over an invisible line, a hidden sniper would fire a well-placed shot to discourage any further intrusion.

MISINTERPRETING YOUR CALLING

The main reason the previous pastor and myself were wounded was that we misinterpreted our calling to this particular church. We were both trained in seminary on the fivefold ministry of: the apostle, the pastor, the teacher, the evangelist, and the prophet. We were trained in the principles of church growth and how to operate within the fivefold ministry. We were also taught about many other giftings, but I never had a class on the office of the assassin. We were taught how to grow a church, but not how to demolish a church in a spiritual manner.

I don't remember attending any classes where the topic of shrinking attendance and its cause was broached. Every one of our professors was adept at growing churches, but I don't remember a single one who was well known for cleaning up messy churches.

I think there should be a class on how to effectively eradicate an entrenched insurgency with minimal collateral damage. There should also be a class on how to survive emotionally while removing the entrenched reprobates who might be residing within the church to which we are assigned.

We do not train our new pastors in military techniques for overcoming entrenched strongholds or fortified positions. The truth is we graduate a lot of protected boys and girls who have not experienced life's hard lessons. We recognize their anointing and present them with ministerial credentials. Then we throw some of them into the lions' den and encourage them to make pets of the lions. I only know one man who ever came out of the lions' den and that was Daniel. We need to remember that before Daniel entered the lions' den, he had first learned how to survive in prison. Our hope is that no pastor will ever be required to enter the lions' den of stiff-necked churches, but the reality is that some will and they need to be equipped to survive.

In a fairly new church, it would be difficult, though not impossible, for insurgents to establish the fortified strongholds we are discussing. The stiff-necked churches I am referring to are well established and have a long history of very successful ministries, but have entered into a prolonged period of spiritual decline. The most telling identifying mark these churches have in common is a recent history of short-termed pastors who have all left, bearing the scars of a devastating battle.

If these anointed pastors were unable to break the strongholds of those churches, then we need to begin dealing differently with the churches. We need to put the safety of our pastors over the contentment of congregations and we need to send in a military-minded man with the personality to eliminate the embedded insurgents.

Another thing these churches have in common is that the foundation is a long-established one. There is a nucleus of people who are and have been the backbone of the church. They will readily tell you that *they* are the reason the church is still standing. They will tell you that regardless of the many mistakes the pastors and staff have made in the past, *they* were the ones who kept the doors open. They will also tell you that regardless of your mistakes, *they* will be faithful to the church. Even if you leave, they will remain until the coming of the Lord. If you quietly search around the church, you will usually find their family names engraved on some pillar. If you are wise, you will never disturb that item without prior approval or you will face the consequences.

These people are the ones who built the foundation and they will let you know they *are* the foundation. If the foundation of the church is solid, then these people can be your greatest asset. If the foundation of the church is lacking, then these people will most likely be your greatest nightmare.

Remember this; if you accept the pastorate of an established church, you also accept the existing foundation. You can do all the research you want, but the church is built on a foundation and you hardly ever see the foundation clearly.

Some people reading this book will say, "Just pray about the church and seek His direction. Ask God if you are to accept the pastorate. Ask God for His direction. If God's answer is yes, accept the pastorate and everything will work out." All of these statements are true. I agree with every one of them. But if these statements are the entire truth, then why do the pastors who follow them complain about problems in the church God assigned them to?

Usually within one or two years, you will start hearing comments like this:

"I couldn't believe the amount of sin I found in the church!"

"The church leaders don't want the church to grow!"

"The people have fought me on every idea!"

"There are two families who think they own the church!"

A lot of other complaints can be made, all dealing with foundational items the pastor was unaware of before taking the assignment. The problems were in the church before the pastor stepped in, but the foundation was hidden from view.

NEW MINISTRY

One of the most exciting times of ministry for me is when a new door of opportunity is opening. It's not that I'm tired of the old ministry, but new adventures bring a renewed excitement. Our whole lives are filled with plateaus and times of change. Sometimes change is good and sometimes it is difficult, but it is always exciting.

I remember the day I was finally old enough to start kindergarten. I left for school filled with excitement over this new stage of my life. I thought this would be a wonderful change. My sister had been going to school for two years. At last, I was joining her. What I expected to be a very enjoyable experience suddenly changed when I came to understand the meaning of the word "bully." I was expecting one set of experiences and my expectations were smashed along with my face.

The question is what do you do when this happens? The pastor comes into his new church expecting to build, and then discovers his ministry is to eradicate part of the church in order to rebuild a strong foundation.

REALITY: RACHEL OR LEAH?

Here's a Bible story that deals with this exact set of circumstances.

Jacob received instructions from his father, Isaac, that it was time for him to seek a wife. He was told not to take a wife from the inhabitants of the land of Canaan. They were not of the seed of Abraham. They served other gods and had strange customs that did not fit into the laws given to Israel by God. Therefore, they were not suitable for marriage. Jacob was told to go to the land of his uncle, Laban, and there he would find a suitable wife.

In obedience to his father, Jacob set out on his journey. As he neared the area where he believed his uncle resided, he asked a local shepherd for the actual location of Laban's camp. The shepherd knew of Laban and directed Jacob's attention to an approaching shepherdess who was one of the daughters of Laban. Jacob took one look at her and immediately did a double take. He found her "beautiful of form and appearance" (Gen. 29:17 NKJV). Jacob went to Rachel, the shepherdess. After identifying himself as a relative, he was invited into Laban's camp, as was the custom of the day.

After a short period of time, Jacob was offered a job. He accepted Laban's offer and started working. After one month, Jacob asked Laban for Rachel's hand in marriage. After some negotiation, Jacob agreed to work for Laban for a total of seven years at which time he would receive Rachel as his wife. At the end of seven years, Jacob approached Laban and reminded him of their agreement. Laban responded by arranging for the marriage to take place.

Scripture does not provide an account of the celebration, but it is obvious it continued well past nightfall. According to the customs of the time, there would have been considerable consumption of wine during the celebration. I have always wondered if the euphoria caused by the festivities and the consumption of wine might have contributed to the events that followed.

After the celebration Jacob entered his tent and waited for Laban to bring Rachel to him. At the appointed time Laban brought his daughter to the tent and gave her to Jacob.

The agreement appeared to be fulfilled. Imagine the level of anticipation Jacob had. He had faithfully served for seven years and now his appointed time had arrived. In the obscurity of darkness he spent the first night with his new wife.

The joy of that night was short lived. In the brightness of morning, Jacob saw clearly.

He immediately confronted Laban and accused him (Gen. 29:25):

So it came to pass in the morning, that behold, it was Leah. And he said to Laban, "What is this you have done to me? Was it not for Rachel that I served you? Why then have you deceived me?" (NKJV)

Jacob went to bed thinking he was married to Rachel and woke up with Leah. Jacob went to bed with his dream and woke up with his reality. His dream lasted one night, but he lived with his reality.

The comparison between this story and pastoring a new church is that sometimes you find your new ministry and your new church are not what you thought they'd be. You thought you were going to be the loving pastor working in unity with the Rachel church. You thought the new church was beautiful "in form and appearance" and that this union was made in heaven.

The union *was* made in heaven. God sent you there, but the church was not a Rachel church, it was a Leah church that you woke up to. God knew all the time that it was a Leah church; you assumed it was a Rachel church.

Many years ago my wife and I accepted an assignment to a small church in a lovely community. The church was beautiful. It had a lot of property with many additional buildings and more than enough parking. My wife and I prayed and we both felt in our hearts we were to accept this new assignment. Our calling was confirmed by all our supervisors and we cheerfully started our new ministry there.

We had just come out of a very tough ministry where we basically did everything. We did the cleaning, the repair work, the financial support, and the evangelism. The people just attended. We were looking forward to working with people who had talent, money, desire, and a great vision to fulfill. Everything these members said to me prior to my assignment sounded like music to my ears. I could finally be *the pastor*. I could finally concentrate on building a church and reaching our new community. I thought ministering with "Rachel" was going to be so much fun.

We started increasing in numbers, almost tripling our attendance in four months. We developed a good staff and everything seemed great… until our first membership meeting. During the meeting approximately ten influential members of the church stood up. One man identified himself as the spokesperson for this group. He said I needed to listen very carefully because they were the financial supporters of that church and the church could not exist without their money. He then told me I needed to stop everything we'd been doing that caused the church to grow. This group was happy with the way things had been done in the past and they were not going to allow change.

I told him the staff and council were all in agreement with the changes and the fruit of the ministry was evidenced by the increase in people. I asked him if they were willing to meet with the leadership and pray about the changes and see if this was God's leading.

He said prayer was not needed. The church was a business, they were the money, and the money dictated what direction the business went.

I was truly shocked. Rachel was beginning to look a lot like Leah.

Over the next few years, I came to realize that the foundation of the church was totally broken and we could not grow until the walls were first demolished and the foundation repaired. The foundation of the church was eaten away by willful, intentional sins, among them greed, pride, dishonesty, sexual perversion, alcoholism, and drug use. These sins were not just manifested in the pews, but they were also in the leadership.

I got a call one Sunday morning from a young man who said he was not a Christian and really did not believe in God, but that something was happening in my church even he felt was not right. He said one of my Sunday school teachers had been partying with him and his friends all night and was drunk and loaded on marijuana and other drugs. This was a weekly occurrence and he did not believe this behavior was right around young children.

I had inherited this reprobate volunteer. He was well-connected with the leading families in the church and had been helping for many years. I went to the Sunday school classroom where he was teaching and took him outside to inquire about what I'd been told. I immediately smelled the odors of marijuana and alcohol on him. I told him he could no longer be a teacher and that I wanted to see him immediately after the morning service.

After I dismissed the service, I went to my office to confront this young man with the hope of restoration. To my surprise, a small group of longtime members waited for me at my office door. Upon seeing me, one person started yelling and demanded that I reinstate the man as the children's Sunday school teacher. I was totally shocked by this behavior and even more shocked when they all admitted they were aware of his behavior but looked past it because he had been doing this teaching for years.

It was about that time I realized I was not there to build the church, but to remove some people so the foundation could be rebuilt. The sins the people engaged in were willful and intentional, and they had refused to change or repent for many years. I realized I had to start thinking like Benaiah and not like Moses.

Moses was required by God to walk with Israel for forty years while they slowly died, but Benaiah achieved the same results in a couple of days. I am not advocating that we always become the assassin. God called Moses to walk with the children of Israel while they slowly died and Benaiah was called to quicken the deaths of the troublemakers, but both men were called by God.

The trick is to know what calling you have received in the church you are appointed to. Are you called to the Moses anointing or the Benaiah anointing? I think a lot of pastors might be walking the Moses walk because no one has ever told them there might be another biblical way.

The oppositional forces in the church previously described were strongly embedded and had no intention of leaving. They had outlasted two or three other pastors and they were planning to outlast me. This had all the earmarks of a prolonged and bloody battle in which many believers would be wounded. The longer a battle continues the more casualties there are. Sometimes the quickest way is the most merciful.

Let's return to my story about the group in the membership meeting and I'll describe what I did after they made their demands. I would never advise or encourage any pastor to do as I did, but it worked for me. After the group spokesman said his piece and it was obvious they were directly challenging my position and authority, I excused myself from the meeting and went into the church office.

After about ten minutes, I slowly and deliberately returned to the meeting. The room was quiet as everyone was wondering where I had gone. I went to the group, looked each one in the eye, and thanked them for coming to the meeting. I then informed them it was a meeting for members only and, being as they were no longer members, they could use the door to exit.

They responded that they were all longtime members and had a right to be in the meeting. I advised them that while I was away from the meeting I had gone to the computer in the church office, highlighted their names on the membership roster, and pushed *delete*. With one push of the button they were no longer on the roster and therefore no longer members.

The atmosphere became icy and cold. We stood staring at each other for a short period of time and then the entire group got up and walked out. In this particular case the action I took worked. The group left and caused no further problems.

For every action, there is an equal and opposite reaction. The reaction to my action was that the group left and took their money with them. Within two or three months we could not pay the church bills. I had to open a contracting business to cover my bills as well as those of the church. For the next nine years, I was a bi-vocational pastor. I worked the construction business during the day and ran the church at night.

The removal of this one group only revealed another level of embedded insurgency. Each level removed revealed another level that had to be dealt with. For this reason, I had to have a second job for nine more years. My mistakes in dealing with this particular church lengthened the amount of time it took to remove the walls and reach the foundation. Because I did not understand the principles of assassination, I tried to walk as Moses when God had called me to walk as Benaiah. Every time I tried to walk patiently and with longsuffering, there were people who would force me to become the assassin and remove them from the church. My authority for these actions is found in 1 Corinthians 5:5:

> Hand this man over to Satan, so that the sinful nature may be destroyed and his spirit saved on the day of the Lord. (NIV)

Sometimes it is just easier to do now what you know will have to be done in the future anyway. Let's just do it!

CHAPTER 3

VULNERABLE SOLDIERS

IT IS IMPORTANT to examine the emotional vulnerability of people who are called into occupations or specific assignments that are not compatible with their emotional makeup. This chapter does not originate from a psychological education but more from experiences drawn from a military and law enforcement background combined with over forty years in ministry.

VICTIMS OF THE INSURGENTS

During the many years I have observed people working in very stressful occupations, I have noticed that many of them survive with their emotions intact while others leave their chosen occupations completely shattered and emotionally broken.

Ministry is one of the most stressful occupations in which a person can work. We all know former ministers who should still be in ministry but are now employed in secular positions. These men and women were wounded unnecessarily and they bear scars that will prevent them from being productive full-time servants of our Lord. We must stop this useless loss of manpower and begin to restore those who have become casualties of battle.

WRONG MAN, WRONG MISSION

This useless destruction of manpower occurs because we assign men and women to specific missions they are not emotionally equipped to perform.

I have found that most pastors are by nature open, loving people who exhibit a high degree of emotional sensitivity. They tend to be very nurturing, overly trusting, and destructively giving of themselves in their dealings with people. These attributes are often manifested to the detriment of themselves and their families.

These same pastors always seem to believe in the innate goodness of mankind, even if they have been betrayed in the past. They seem to have an inner voice telling them that even the worst reprobate really wants to become a valuable asset to society. They believe that given the time, the opportunity, and the encouragement, everyone is willing and able to change for good. These pastors are filled with mercy and seem to have an unlimited amount of patience and longsuffering, but there are situations when they fail miserably because of these very same traits.

There are two men in the Bible who immediately come to my mind when I consider these attributes: King David and Moses. King David was so merciful he left problems for Solomon to clean up. Moses was so merciful he walked with the stiff-necked people for forty years.

These merciful pastors will walk with their congregations for years and maybe even die with them, but these same pastors are emotionally vulnerable when it comes to a situation where the intentional elimination of a church member is required. They may take the necessary action, but they'll suffer emotional trauma as they operate outside the parameters of their natural strengths. I will refer to this group of merciful and longsuffering pastors as the David or Moses anointing.

There is another group of pastors who, though smaller in number, are also anointed. This second group of pastors I will refer to as the Solomon or Benaiah anointing. This anointing can best be described by looking at the actions of Solomon and Benaiah after they were made aware of the problems remaining in King David's realm.

Once David instructed Solomon to eradicate Shimei and Joab, Solomon wasted no further time. He immediately assigned this task to Benaiah, who immediately set about eliminating these men. In short order the job was completed and the problem was solved.

It is obvious that the David/Moses anointing has a totally different personality and emotional makeup from the Solomon/Benaiah anointing. Both are called by God but they are called to different ministries and their ministries have very different outcomes.

Special Forces

When I was in the military I got to know many soldiers who joined special operations units. It did not take long to realize these special ops soldiers marched to the beat of a different drummer. The ones I met were extremely loyal, dedicated, and faithful to their callings, but there was also something in their character that made them different—unique. They could be in a crowd of a thousand people, but they would not exactly fit in. In fact, many of these special ops soldiers really did not want to become like the standard regimented soldier. They truly enjoyed being different.

The special ops soldiers seemed to operate best in small, intimate units consisting of four to six members. They did not need a large gathering of soldiers to validate their possibilities of success. Soldiers who seemed to possess the unique combination of emotions and personalities needed to operate in these special units were few and far between.

I believe I can safely say these special ops soldiers possessed the same personality as the assassin I described in the previous chapters. These soldiers operated almost totally by logic and seemed to thrive in stressful and dangerous situations. I don't know if the dangerous situations found them or if they found the dangerous situations, but the two always seemed to be together.

I believe the Benaiah pastor would more closely fit the mold of the Special Forces soldier than the regimented soldier. Both the Benaiah pastor and the Special Forces soldier operate from logic and have the unique ability to separate their emotions from their duties.

The main point is that it takes an unusual type of person to survive this special ministry of removing insurgents who are deeply entrenched within the fibers of a church body. Our failure to recognize these different types of ministries and the unique personality combinations required in each of the different offices has resulted in casualties that could have been avoided.

MOST QUALIFIED

When we are forced to deal with a problem church that has defeated every pastor who has been sent there, we look for the most "qualified" and experienced pastor. The pastor we send might be well qualified to plant or grow a church, but he probably never had to demolish one. This makes him a novice in this unique ministry. His lack of experience does not disqualify him from assuming the pastorate of a troubled church, and it does not mean he lacks the ability, but having pastored growing churches also does not automatically mean he's qualified to dismantle a troubled church.

The fact that we do not recognize the "assassin" pastor or the "demolishing" pastor means we have not identified the necessary leadership to effectively and safely remove insurgents; therefore we are limited in our ability to react to embedded insurgents.

In the military, this situation would be like sending a forward observer on a mission that required an airborne soldier. The forward observer has never been trained to jump from an airplane; yet if we were to send him to jump, we would be asking him to perform a dangerous mission without the benefit of intense training.

The truth of the matter is, the parachute *might* open; the forward observer *might* make it to the ground in one piece, and he *might* still be able to walk, at which time it might seem we made a wise and correct decision. The reality is that we may have simply been extremely lucky with the outcome.

The opposite is also a possibility. The forward observer might have jumped from the plane and his parachute *might not* have opened and he *might not* have known how to open his reserve chute and he would still be falling. The reality is that he would make it to the ground, but he would not be in one piece and he would not be able to walk after he got there.

I have never known a military commander who would assign a man to a mission without first analyzing the special requirements necessary and handpicking the specific soldier with the best chance of successfully completing and surviving that mission.

Wolves Among The Sheep

I think we often forget that a church can be the enemy's playground. Paul refers to this in Acts 20:29-31:

> For I know this, that after my departing shall grievous wolves enter in among you, not sparing the flock. Also of your own selves, shall arise, speaking perverse things, to draw away disciples after them. Therefore watch, and remember, that by the space of three years I ceased not to warn every one night and day with tears. (KJV)

Because of his unique personality combination, Paul would most likely fit the mold of an assassin pastor. He was not afraid of confrontation and did not hesitate to eliminate reprobates when necessary. This fact is shown throughout his letters. More than once he warned the troublemakers that he would soon be at their churches and would be dealing harshly with them.

Paul is the same man who recommended that a habitual sinner be turned over to Satan for the destruction of the flesh so his soul might be salvaged. Paul was like Solomon; he took care of problems without wasting time. Paul was speaking to the church at Ephesus when he wrote the above passage, but it is meant for every church. Satan will send wolves (insurgents) in his attempt to destroy the vibrant church. The wolves will infiltrate the church by appearing to be sheep and will wreak havoc until they are exposed and driven from the flock. Paul instructs the shepherd to watch for the wolves that try to infiltrate from outside the local church. He also warns that wolves will rise up from within the church.

The wolf is in the church for one reason and that is to devour the sheep. The protector of the sheep is the pastor who is led by the Holy Spirit and is empowered to remove the wolves. Not all pastors are equally equipped to remove the well-entrenched wolf that has convinced the sheep he is one of them. Whether we call them wolves, moles, insurgents, termites, or just plain habitual troublemakers, the solution is still the same. Extreme cases require the forced expulsion of these members.

There is a surefire method for determining if a wolf is present among the sheep. If the sheep keep disappearing or suffering injuries, then we must assume something other than a sheep is present. If the shepherd keeps coming up injured or missing, then we must assume there is one mean wolf in the flock. One way to get rid of a mean wolf is to send in a meaner shepherd.

If there is a predator in the flock, you don't send a sheep to fight it. I don't care how mean the sheep is, it will still be devoured. If you want to destroy a predator, you must send in an experienced hunter and not a merciful shepherd.

Too often we send in David shepherds to fulfill the ministry of a Benaiah. If we continue to operate in this manner we will continue to lose qualified pastors who are needed to build our thriving churches.

FIGHTING ALONE

Saul knew the exact situation he was sending David into when he sent him to battle against Goliath. He knew Goliath was an experienced man of war, who had killed many warriors far better trained than David. Saul knew only a miracle could save David.

Saul was hoping for a miracle, but he wasn't really expecting one. If you remember, Saul tried to give David his own personal armor. Saul's actions showed his real level of faith. He would not have given his armor to David if he were planning to use it himself. Saul had absolutely no intention of entering the battle or coming to David's aid if things went bad. Saul told David, "Go and the Lord be with you." The reason Saul said, "The Lord be with you," was that Saul would not be there and neither would any of the other soldiers. The only person who might be with David was the Lord.

I believe another reason Saul tried to give his armor away was because the weight of the armor would have slowed him down. If David was killed, Saul planned on making a hasty retreat and the armor would only be a hindrance to his escape. He only needed the armor if he was planning on entering the battle.

I wonder what would have happened if Saul and the rest of the Israelites had left their foxholes and stood beside David as he faced the giant. God still could have used David and the battle still would have been won, but David would not have had to face the giant alone. Many times we as leaders do the same thing to our pastors.

DEVELOPING A BATTLE PLAN

Even if we know a church has a proven history of killing or wounding pastors, we continue to send pastors in alone and without so much as a battle plan. Why not sit down with these pastors first and through prayer and planning develop a battle plan? A battle plan lets all the members of the team know the exact situation they face and the most effective course of action.

When we select the right pastor and present him with a well-developed course of action that should remedy the problem situation, we enter the battle with him. Even if we are not there physically when the insurgents make their attack, the pastor knows we've got his back.

This principle was proven in my life many years ago in the early 1970s when I was working a one-man car for a local police department. I was assigned to a gang area where there was a large apartment complex called the Pueblo.

I had heard that gangs claimed to rule the complex, selling guns and drugs door to door, so I decided to initiate a foot patrol at the Pueblo. During a slow time of the day, I left the car and started my walk through. As I neared the center of the complex, I was confronted by a group of gang members who told me I had no right to enter "their" complex and they would kill me if I ever came into it again.

I told them I'd be back in one hour and I would again start walking the complex. I let them know I would be alone and if they wanted to "get it on, then let's get it on." I left the area, met with a sergeant, and told him what I wanted to do. I think he was just as crazy as I was because he said to go ahead. We arranged for the sergeant to be in the area of the Pueblo, but to remain out of sight. He would position himself so he could hear any gunshots and would have the necessary backup available to come to my aid if anything went down.

I drove back, parked my police car, and started walking the Pueblo. To my surprise, the good people who lived in the complex began to tell me where the gangs were waiting to ambush me. Because of this information, I was able to circle around the gangs and the situation ended with them backing down and temporarily leaving the complex. To act in such a manner today would get me a room in the mental hospital, but in those days, it got me the Police Officer of the Year Award and $25.

I must confess I was extremely nervous when I entered the complex alone, but I had comfort knowing the support of the entire police department was only a block away if I needed it. As you can see, it is easier to hold the fort against the enemy if you know the cavalry is right around the corner.

What is the problem with saying we need a knowledgeable assassin rather than a longsuffering shepherd? We are simply acknowledging a situation that we don't like to talk about. It's about time we bring this situation out of the closet and into the family room so it can be dealt with as a family.

Many years ago I was set to become the pastor of a long-established church when the supervisor asked me a question I will never forget. He asked if I wanted to close the doors of the church for six months and then start anew.

I knew the church had some problems, but I had no idea how serious they were. Obviously, this leader knew more about what was going on than I did. If he was willing to close the entire church down, then the problems were extreme. He did not share any details with me. In retrospect, I should have asked why he thought such a drastic move was necessary, but I was young and filled with zeal. I thought I could work through any problems that existed. He did not volunteer any information, and I did not ask.

I must assume full responsibility for my mistakes in this situation because I saw things that troubled me, but I never pursued them. On the other hand, my superiors also saw problem areas, but they never communicated them to me either. Due to this series of mistakes and miscommunications, I felt I had been sent into battle to face the giant alone. Everyone knew severe problems existed, but no one took the time to discuss them or to jointly seek a solution.

I went into this church expecting growth, but experienced prolonged decline. I know the same situation has happened to other pastors and many of them have gone through the same roller coaster of emotions that I did. There were two basic areas in which the enemy attacked me: isolation and failure.

INTERNAL ISOLATION

One of the first emotions a battling pastor might experience is isolation, which comes from both internal and external sources. The feeling of being isolated is not a sudden thing. It develops over a period of months or even years.

Let's say you are with a group of fellow pastors or close friends when someone asks the typical question. "How is everything going at your new church?"

Everyone is excited about your new assignment so they wait expectantly for your answer. You now have a choice to make. You can either lie and say, "Great," which is the path many choose to follow, or you can be truthful and say, "Not good."

If you choose to be honest, your friends will immediately express concern and rally around you. They will listen intently and offer much heartfelt advice and prayer. The next few times this occurs, they will still express interest, but you'll notice their response is less enthusiastic. Their interest is quickly drawn into other areas and their interaction with you is limited. Eventually, when this group asks how you're doing, it will be out of courtesy rather than concern. By that time you simply lie and answer, "Great." You have now become isolated.

For whatever reason, you make the decision not to share with your fellow pastors the continued trials you are battling. Your reason for not sharing could be embarrassment, a sense of failure, emotional exhaustion, or any one of a dozen other reasons, but the result is the same. You shut out your friends, internalize your struggles, and fight the battle alone.

External Isolation

The other source of isolation is external.

Some people are so self-consumed they just don't have the time or interest to be concerned about you or your problem. The sad part is that some of these self-consumed people are your fellow pastors. They are so busy building their own ministries they only care about what is happening within their own walls.

If this is the group with whom you are trying to share, you will never break through their wall of self-success. They will isolate you because you have nothing to offer them. They will smile, give you a pat on the head, and a religious saying such as, "We will pray for you," or "Go, and the Lord be with you," but their only thoughts are on their own ministries. They have just isolated you.

FAILURE

Another feeling that often accompanies isolation is failure. One of the main topics of conversation when pastors get together is the status of their churches. There are certain buzzwords connected to this topic that will stimulate conversation and others that put a definite damper on any enthusiastic interaction. Some of the words everyone wants to hear are growth, increase, new families, expanding programs, revival, and powerful new staff. On the other hand, if you want to stifle the conversation, just mention decreased attendance, financial hardship, rebellious staff, or any other phrase that might indicate discouragement or non-clinical depression on the part of the pastor.

I remember one phrase I heard so often when I was an evangelist that I shudder even now when I think of it. I would ask a pastor how his church was doing and he would reply, "God is sifting the congregation again." This usually meant the church was once more reduced to only him and his family. This was a guaranteed conversation blocker.

In these types of conversations, you will often find the majority of pastors are experiencing growth and blessings while you are experiencing death and destruction. These blessed pastors rush to their churches on Sunday morning to see how many new families have come in while you force yourself to go to church to see how many more have left. You begin to wonder what you are doing wrong. Your thoughts are that if everyone else is experiencing growth, then you should be too.

You remember the church growth seminars all these successful pastors were talking about. They gave credit to the seminars for their new growth so you decide to give it a try. By faith you start attending all the seminars. You read all the new books on church growth and you immediately implement all these proven church growth tools in your ministry. To your great amazement, your church continues to die.

It would seem that even with proven church growth tools, *you* are unable to change the downward spiral of your church. After a short time, it becomes painfully obvious that the problem is not the tools. The problem must be you. You begin to ask yourself what is wrong with you. You wonder what you're doing wrong. Certain questions begin to haunt you.

I am not talking about hypothetical questions; I am talking about real life experiences. I have spoken to pastors who experienced these same circumstances and they've shared the questions they asked themselves.

One pastor had to battle the question of whether or not he was really "called" to that particular church. He knew he was called to pastoral ministry and that he was to be the senior pastor of a church, but was this right one?

"If this was the right church for me to pastor, shouldn't it be growing?"

Another pastor questioned whether he should be the senior pastor or maybe just a staff member. The enemy attacked him on his ability to lead a congregation. He began to think that maybe he should have been the youth pastor, Sunday school superintendent, or in some other area of ministry, but not the leader of the congregation. His thinking was that surely a leader would know how to bring a church into renewed growth. Growth is always the objective, so a leader must have the qualities needed to accomplish this task.

The hardest question anyone shared with me was the one that brought the greatest anguish to these pastors. "Did I really pray enough?" I heard this more than any other question and it probably caused the most pastors to leave their churches. It's definitely a killer question. Every pastor knows he or she could, and should, pray more. We know the importance of prayer and we desire to pray more, but our daily duties keep us from spending twenty-four hours a day in prayer.

Because of our mind-set in this area, the question quickly finds fertile ground and takes root. The problem is compounded by the testimonies of other pastors who faced seemingly the same set of circumstances and, through a regimen of intense prayer, were able to break through.

With these thoughts in mind, we drop everything else we were doing and enter into an intense period of prayer and fasting. We dedicate weeks, maybe even months, to this regimen of prayer. The church still does not grow and it soon becomes obvious to us that we are the problem. Realizing this, the best course of action is to get rid of the problem, so we resign. After we leave the church, a new pastor takes over, and here is the surprise: The new pastor has the same problem.

As it turns out, the problem was not the type of leadership nor was it the type of program. The problem was that there were wolves (insurgents) among the sheep. The wolves were planting seeds of rebellion, resulting in a stiff-necked people who would die in the wilderness unless the wolves were eliminated from the flock.

Pastors continually assume they are the problem because they are thinking like a "pastor." They need to quit thinking like a victim and begin thinking like an assassin. We must identify and eliminate the problem that holds back growth. We need to stop thinking like Moses and start thinking like Benaiah.

The embedded insurgents are going to leave the church eventually, so why not speed up the process in a godly and biblical way? The wolves need to be eliminated and not allowed to die of old age or from overeating sheep. Fewer people will be hurt by a speedier process. There must be a change in our thought process if we are to save our pastors.

CHAPTER 4

ARMED RESISTANCE

WHEN I WAS a younger man, I used to joke with my friends about the "old people" who always seemed to be reading *National Geographic* magazine. It was something "older people" did.

My wife reminds me of this when she walks into the room and sees me watching the National Geographic television show or tuned into the Explorer Channel. I try to convince her I'm simply doing research for my books and I'm really not enjoying the show. Now, though, I finally have the chance to use some examples from the programs that I watched.

THE GREATEST DEFENSE IS AN OVERWHELMING OFFENSE

One of the many things I've noticed on these shows is the protective nature of a female guarding her nest.

The nest contains the eggs of the unborn young that are the mother's most valuable asset. She will defend her young even at the cost of her own life. Most of the mothers seem to defend their young by mounting an overwhelming offense. When a predator approaches the nest or comes within a certain predefined area, the female senses danger and attacks the predator. The attack is so overwhelming, the predator will leave her young alone and seek easier prey.

The greatest defense is often a powerful offense. In the military, a black ops unit functions in much the same way. They remain hidden by blending in with their surroundings. They use camouflage to change their appearance and seem to be just part of the scenery. Most people would not even know they are there. If compromised, they will attack with overwhelming firepower and ferocity. When the enemy takes cover, they will attempt to break contact and disappear back into the jungle where they immediately change their appearance and once again blend in. These units use hit-and-run tactics because they are unable to maintain a prolonged battle against superior numbers.

The same attitude is prevalent in human nature. We often attack people we consider a threat to the things we value. This happens even if what we value will eventually destroy our church, our families, or us. We will still defend it even unto death. This action defies logic. Many times the things we value most are the very things keeping us from achieving success, fulfillment, and happiness.

In many churches, eggs have been laid in the nests of destruction that will prevent the church from entering its promised land. These eggs might be immorality, power, control, comfort, racial separation, or a multitude of other destructive values that are protected by the members. They own the eggs, therefore, they will defend them against anyone considered to be a threat.

Uniting Against The Pastor

If a new pastor approaches the sacred nests of a church, the defenders unite and attack that pastor. The defenders may not even like each other, but they will unite against the outsider.

As a police officer, I knew one of the most dangerous calls to respond to was a family disturbance. One night I was sent to such a call. Two brothers were fighting in the street in front of their home. It was actually a member of the family who placed the call.

As I arrived on the scene, I saw the two men in the middle of the street engaged in a fistfight. I attempted to separate them and I immediately became the focus of their anger. They stopped fighting each other and began attacking me. I was there to help them at the request of their family. I was there to keep them from hurting each other, but I became the target of their attack.

If the two brothers had just admitted they were wrong and had stopped the fighting, the problem could easily have been solved. Instead, it escalated to the point that both men, along with five additional family members who joined them, were all charged with felonious assault on a police office and went to jail.

As the authority figure, I suffered cuts and bruises because I was doing my job and got too close to the family protecting the nest of eggs. In response to my presence they circled the wagons and attempted to protect the very situation that was destroying the family. The same response often occurs in a problem church.

The overseers assign a new pastor with the intent of restoring health to a body in the midst of self-destructive behavior. The pastor enters the situation as the authority figure and is instantly seen as a threat to the status quo—a danger to the protected eggs that have been laid within the fibers of that church. In response, the members will often circle the wagons and attack anyone who attempts to venture within the confines of that sacred land.

The new pastor is seen as a threat, so the members launch a vicious attack with the intent of protecting the very sin that has been destroying the church. They will operate in much the same manner as a black ops unit in the military. They will try to remain hidden so they can continue to sow their seeds of destruction unobstructed. They will use religious camouflage so they appear to be a valuable part of the church structure.

If the new pastor confronts them, they will attack with great ferocity in their attempt to intimidate him.

If he backs off or hesitates in his mission to cleanse the church, this subversive element will break off its attack and attempt to infiltrate the healthy segment of the church and once again operate with impunity.

There are occasions when a new pastor is so overcome by the suddenness and ferocity of the attack that he will not venture into these dangerous areas again in hopes that the insurgents will disappear forever.

The divisive elements of a church will often provide a united front when any of them are confronted. Just as the family of the two fighting brothers united and attacked me when I was a police officer, so also will the divisive elements in the church unite even if they dislike each other.

I am reminded of a situation that took place while Jesus was being crucified, recorded in Luke 23:12.

> That very day Pilate and Herod became friends with each other, for previously they had been at enmity with each other. (NKJV)

Pilate and Herod formed a friendship based on their united efforts against Jesus.

Hidden Insurgency

The outward appearance of a church often belies its true spiritual nature. The church may appear to be a healthy group of people gathered to worship the

Lord, while in reality it is a hotbed of insurgents just waiting for the right moment to spring their attack.

Remember the earlier example of the black ops unit? These units use camouflage to remain hidden while they perform their special assignments. In a church, the members who are responsible for the greatest damage often appear to be the most spiritual. They are experts at using religious camouflage. They often volunteer for important and powerful positions within the church such as council president, treasurer, Sunday school superintendent, intercession leader, praise leader, or even youth leader.

These people often hide behind religious rhetoric. They are notorious for using phrases such as, "Let us pray," "God told me," or even, "Let's just persevere through the problem." How can you debate a person whose conversation starts with, "God told me," especially when he or she is well entrenched within the church?

The pastor is a newcomer who has no track record within the church. If he were to counter with the phrase, "God told me something different," you already know whom they will believe. It won't be the new guy.

Remember, we are not talking about a healthy church. We are talking about a very dysfunctional church and so the response won't be normal. These subversive elements, which masquerade as spiritual giants, will even correctly identify the spiritual problem but then point to innocent people as the cause.

This is a great way to misdirect the investigation. An example of this is another event that occurred while I was a police detective.

One of my friends was assigned to make an undercover buy at a well-known drug house. This particular house was run by a very violent and experienced gang. Many times our undercover officers wore wireless devices to record conversations and to let us know if anything was wrong. What we didn't know was that the gang at this particular drug house had installed an alarm system that would sound when a wireless device was detected.

As our detective reached the walkway, another individual came up alongside him, apparently there to buy drugs. As both men reached the front door, the wireless our man was wearing set off the alarm. The undercover officer instantly responded and yelled, "Snitch!" and grabbed the man beside him. Everyone in the house jumped on this poor guy while our detective walked away.

The dealers never realized they had the wrong guy because we rushed in and pulled this drug user out. Everyone assumed the drug user was the "snitch" because the real narc identified him as such. In the dealers' rush to judgment they accepted this faulty identification. In the church world, the real troublemaker will often falsely identify an innocent person in order to maintain his or her subversive work and remain in a position of authority.

CHAPTER 5

A MOLE IN THE UNIT

WEBSTER'S NEW STUDENT *Dictionary* defines the word "mole" as "any of numerous burrowing insectivores with tiny eyes, concealed ears, and soft fur." Based on this definition of a mole in the animal kingdom, a mole might be considered somewhat cute and rather harmless.

Another usage of the word "mole" describes a human who exhibits attributes similar to the mole of the animal kingdom. The human mole is rarely seen, but the aftermath of his presence is always recognized by the trail of destruction left behind.

Throughout the history of the intelligence community, moles have been used to infiltrate secretive enemy units and render them ineffective.

Two Methods Used By The Mole

One way the mole can destroy a unit is to reveal its secret operating information to the enemy. The second method is to plant false information within the intelligence unit so they spend their time following false trails.

By examining how moles were used during World War II or the Cold War between Russia and the United States, we see how effective they can be. Throughout the Cold War Russia planted many moles within the units that were gathering intelligence about Russia. These units were themselves using spies, double agents, and moles to gather their information. In some cases the moles were able to infiltrate these units and identify the spies we were using. By revealing this information they were able to destroy the effectiveness of the mission. In other cases the moles would plant false information intended to neutralize the effectiveness of the unit by causing them to chase false leads. At still other times they would publish misinformation that would cause our leaders to make wrong decisions.

The success of a mole was centered in his or her ability to burrow deep within the inner circle of a unit and gain the confidence of the leaders. The mole had to appear like one of the most loyal employees and keep all of his or her movements above suspicion.

This tried-and-true method has been employed throughout the history of war or conflict and has proven to be very successful. Today, the mole is even used in the business sector to obtain secrets from competing companies.

A struggling business will, on occasion, assign an employee the task of hiring on to a competitor's company with the sole intent of stealing trade secrets. On the surface the employee is working for the new company, but in reality he is taking his orders from his true employer. His job is not to make a profit for the new company, but to benefit the company that sent him in as a mole. You would never send a mole into a failing business. You would only send a mole into a company on the cutting edge of technology or with trade secrets worth stealing.

In the military you would never send a mole into a country you did not consider a threat. The United States and Russia infiltrated each other because we considered each other a threat to the safety and well-being of our individual nations. Russia was promoting communism and the United States was promoting democracy. The two were in direct contrast to each other. These two ideologies could not co-exist because they were diametrically opposed to each other. Therefore, we each used moles to try to undermine the opposition.

THE CHURCH

The church is often referred to as the army of God. The Bible often uses terms such as "our weapons" or "our armor." We know a war is raging between the forces of good and the forces of evil, between light and darkness, between life and death, and in its final form, between God and Satan.

Satan wants to rule this world and the only force stopping him is the army of God, also called the "church." Satan is referred to as the "prince" of the power of the air, but he will not be happy until he becomes the "king."

The church is at war. The battle is taking place within our churches and the soldiers are the members of our congregations. The only way Satan can win the war is to destroy our churches and the only way he can do that is by infiltrating them and planting moles within the church structure.

A Dead Target Is Never Attacked

The churches under attack are ones Satan sees as a threat. We know from the first three chapters of the book of Revelation that some churches are already spiritually dead. Some have lost their first love and others have become glorified social clubs where the Word of God is never shared. They would probably deny that a battle is taking place. And from their viewpoint, they are probably right.

In all my studies on various wars, I have never heard of an army that planned and staged an attack on its own prisoner of war camp. For Satan to attack some of our churches would be like an army attacking its own prison camp. The enemy is already inside and the church is unarmed and defeated. Why would you attack something you have already defeated?

Satan will concentrate on targets he views as a threat. He will attack churches that are actively fulfilling the Great Commission. He will attack churches that have a vision and are actively pursuing that vision.

The size of the church is not the measuring stick by which Satan judges the threat against his kingdom. The measuring stick is the potential of a church. If a church possesses the heart of God, then that church is a threat regardless of size, and it had better realize it is at war.

The Importance of Each Church

Every church is important for the successful completion of God's overall battle plan. Every church has a specific mission and all these missions, when seen as a whole, comprise the overall battle plan.

There are approximately thirty-three individual churches within my city. Some critics might say that's too many churches for a small town of only 55,000 people. If we view them as competitors, then thirty-three churches are too many. But if we view them as co-workers, then each one becomes important. I believe that every Bible-believing, God-fearing church is part of God's overall battle plan and has a very specific mission and a reason for being in the city.

In the military you have battalion-size units and you have small teams consisting of six to eight members all under one command. The battalion and the teams are equally important and are not based on size, but on specialty. There are certain missions a team can accomplish that a battalion cannot. Likewise, there are missions only a battalion or a company can accomplish. In God's army there are also battalions (mega churches) and teams (small churches), but each is important to the overall success of God's battle plan.

The success of each church, be it large or small, is important to the overall success of God's battle plan and each success is interrelated. Many times the mega churches are so concerned with their own vision they couldn't care less about the smaller churches. The smaller churches, on the other hand, are so jealous of the mega churches that any bad news is good news. As Paul the apostle said, "Brethren, these things ought not to be." Or as Rodney King from Los Angeles said, "Can't we all just get along?"

Each individual church, regardless of size, has a specific mission and it is important to the overall battle plan.

Specific Missions

In the military, the battle plan is drawn up by the highest ranking officer. He looks at all the individual units under his command and based on his available manpower, he and his advisors formulate a plan that includes every unit at his disposal.

The battle plan is then broken down into missions that are assigned to various units under his command. Some missions might require thousands of soldiers and other missions might require six or seven soldiers, but each mission is important to the overall success of the battle plan.

Each unit is acutely aware that the success of its specific mission is intertwined with the success of the other units. No one unit operates independently of the other units. It might be unaware of the specific missions assigned to the other units, but it knows how important the other units' missions are. Every specific mission not accomplished weakens the entire battle plan and endangers the operation. There is some unidentified point at which the combined failures of the specific missions will cause catastrophic failure of the battle plan as a whole.

The point is that every specific mission, regardless of the size of the unit, is of utmost importance to the success of the battle plan. God is our General. He formulates the battle plan and communicates it to the churches through Jesus Christ, who is the head of the church. The day-to-day operations have been given to the Holy Spirit. The chain of command has been established and set over the churches.

Satan knows the only weaknesses in God's army are the individual churches. He knows if he can defeat enough of the churches, he can derail the battle plan. We know Satan cannot win the battle but he can sure wreak havoc with the specific missions.

DIVIDE AND CONQUER

The real success of the mega churches rests in the support and success of the small churches. At the same time, the success of the small churches rests in the support and success of the mega churches. This is not success based upon numbers, notoriety, or finances that are the standard parameters by which we typically judge success. I am talking about the successful completion of the Great Commission as given by Jesus Christ.

Satan places moles within our churches to destroy the battle plan God has developed. These moles work in the background and one of their goals is to divide the churches so he can conquer the warriors, church by church.

Generals have long used the divide and conquer tactic as part of their battle plans. I remember hearing about the pincher movements of World War II that cut off units from their support units. Once divided, the separated units were literally fighting for their lives.

During the Vietnam War we often tried to destroy the supply lines that provided food, weapons, and support to the soldiers fighting against our men. One of the failures of the Vietnam War was that we were unable to completely destroy these vital links and therefore were unable to defeat the enemy unit by unit. The units fighting our troops were no match for the military might of our combined forces and we would have won the war if we had been able to remain united and break the unity of the enemy.

The enemy could not defeat our troops on the ground, nor could they divide them, but they did win when they were able to divide the support system in the United States. By causing division among the citizens, politicians, and soldiers, the enemy was able to undermine the determination and unity of our fighting men. By doing this, it was able to win the war.

This is not to say whether the Vietnam War was right or wrong. We simply need to look at the enemy's tactics because what worked once will most likely work again. Our enemy, Satan, is smart enough to know that this tactic worked in the secular world and it will also work in the spiritual world because men and women are fighting the battle.

Satan knows if he can divide the churches, he can stop any support system that has developed. Satan is too wise to openly cause war between churches and denominations, even though he has already been successful at that. Instead, he operates in a far more subtle way.

Every pastor probably knows the parable in Luke 10:30-37 by heart. A man was traveling from Jerusalem to Jericho. During his trip, robbers attacked him, stole his money, and left him almost dead. Later a priest came upon the man but walked by on the other side of the road. Next, a Levite came upon him and he also walked by on the other side. The last person to come by was a Samaritan. He stopped, gave aid to this injured man, and paid for his care while he recovered.

Jesus' final words were, "Go and do likewise."

I have often wondered why Jesus used members of the religious community as the people who turned their backs on the injured man rather than merchants or people in other secular fields. After thinking about it, I finally realized that he *did* use someone in a secular field and he was the one who stopped and helped.

Every pastor preaches from this text, but I wonder how many actually practice what they preach when it comes to the churches within their city. We help some churches, especially if the struggling pastor is from our own denomination or is a personal friend. But the parable is not talking about friends or denominations. The parable is talking about a relationship that was adversarial by nature.

The Samaritan man crossed cultural and political barriers to reach out and help this wounded man. The Samaritan was truly a good neighbor.

The Battle is "Ours" Not "Theirs"

Joshua 1:13-15 gives a clear example of how churches were intended to work together and support each other.

> Remember the word which Moses the servant of the Lord commanded you, saying, "The Lord your God is giving you rest and is giving you this land." Your wives, your little ones, and your livestock shall remain in the land which Moses gave you on this side of the Jordan. But you shall pass before your brethren armed, all your mighty men of valor, and help them, until the Lord has given your brethren rest, as He gave you, and they

also have taken possession of the land which the Lord your God is giving them. Then you shall return to the land of your possession and enjoy it, which Moses the Lord's servant gave you on this side of the Jordan toward the sunrise. (NKJV)

The Israelites were divided into various tribes and each was given a portion of land. This is like the various churches in a city. Each church operates like a tribe and each church has a territory to conquer and control, but they still belong to the same army.

The tribes that had already conquered their territory were instructed not to rest until their brethren had also conquered their own territories. They were instructed to stand alongside them and to send their mighty men to fight for their brothers' possessions. They were to sacrifice until their brothers also entered into rest. Imagine if all the churches in one city started working together to make sure that each church was winning its specific mission. There would be unity instead of a "divide and conquer" mentality. What would happen if we pastors quit being competitors and started being friends?

There was a large church in a rather small city that had been so blessed in the area of music that it had five professional-quality praise and worship teams. The church used one main team and then every eight or nine weeks one of the other teams would lead praise and worship. This meant that every Sunday four of the teams were not being used to minister.

In that same city there were other churches that had no musicians and either praised to CDs or praised without music. We all know how important praise is to the flow of the service. When praise and worship are struggling, the entire service seems to struggle.

I was not in that city, but I wondered how hard it would have been for the blessed pastor to share his extra praise and worship teams with other churches in his own city. I have asked this question of numerous pastors and without exception each one responded with excuses. One pastor said he couldn't help because he had no idea what churches in his city had special needs. My response to him was, "How sad." Another pastor told me he didn't have time to meet the other pastors in his city and therefore had no idea what was happening outside his own church. My response to him was, "How sad."

HEROES

In the military, heroes are the men who don't find reasons something *won't* work, they find a way to *make it* work. In God's army and in the battle against the forces of Satan, we are desperately in need of some heroes.

King Saul was desperately in need of a hero when his armies were facing Goliath. He had a lot of good soldiers who were convinced no one could defeat the giant. Only one man was willing to find a way. When David stood up and advanced on Goliath, God made a way and the enemy was defeated. God only made a way after David walked in faith and stepped into the battle. God won't make a way as long as we remain negative and hide in the foxholes.

The point of all these examples is that the church body is really a divided body where each church fights its own battles and the surviving churches divvy up the surviving sheep. To pacify ourselves we call this church growth. God's battle plan is being compromised because individual churches are losing their specific missions. We need to start working together as an army rather than letting the enemy divide and conquer.

A Mole in My Church

Another tactic used by the enemy to conquer churches is to plant moles within the church leadership. A mole will most often be trained and equipped for a specific ministry that is of utmost importance to the growth of the church. It will usually be in an area the church has struggled with and this mole will appear to be a great blessing. In reality he is a curse sent by Satan directly from the pit of hell.

My wife and I were assigned to what was described to us as a "dying church." When we arrived, we found the church was not dying, it was already dead. No one attended that church and in a town of two thousand, no one seemed interested in attending, either. To support ourselves and the church, my brother and I started a construction company and we worked the jobs together with our wives.

The construction company was doing exceptionally well, which meant we were working ten to twelve hours a day. My wife and I also maintained a full schedule of services at the church and soon it began to grow. Attendance reached sixty people, requiring more time on our part for janitorial, administrative, and ministry work.

We were both reaching the point of total exhaustion when a couple who had been faithfully attending the church for a few months requested a meeting with us. This couple was retired and wanted to become more involved in ministry. They believed God had sent them to our church. They had received formal training in a Bible school and the references they gave were all positive. They were willing to do anything around the church to enable my wife and me to be free to minister to the people.

We reached an agreement whereby this couple would do the maintenance, the repairs, and the cleaning of the church, and my wife and I would do the "ministry." They were faithful in their assignments so my wife and I had some free time to reach out to the community. The church continued to grow and I thought what a great blessing this couple was to the church and to us.

This blessing lasted for almost six months when the mole finally surfaced. The couple eventually came to me and said they had been meeting privately with some members who were concerned about the future of the church. They informed me that during their private times of prayer, God had come to this group and told them that I should start doing the maintenance, repairs, and cleanup because I was better at the physical aspects of ministry and they should start doing the spiritual ministry.

Because I was holding down a secular job, they didn't think I had the necessary time to prepare for ministry and because they were retired they did have the time. They said I could keep the title of senior pastor, but they would start doing the spiritual ministry, including the preaching and teaching. It turned out that while I was working away from the church, this couple had been planting seeds of rebellion and were actively trying to undermine my authority and my position. The mole had burrowed deeply into some very strategic areas.

The moles in a church are the people who have listened to the lies of Satan and have willfully and intentionally made a decision to follow a plan of action that would hinder or subvert the specific mission of a church. A mole is planted by Satan with intent and forethought. A mole does not just happen.

Satan is a master counterfeiter. We know his ability because the Bible describes him as coming like an "angel of light." He knows how to make a mole look like a sheep.

Summary

There is a war raging and the battle is taking place in our churches. Satan has every intention of stopping the church and he does it by planting moles whose every intention is to bring division within the church and ultimately bring division between churches. We must operate as an army to locate and defeat the moles Satan has planted and we can do this through the unity brought by the Holy Spirit.

CHAPTER 6

ROOTING OUT THE MOLE

A MOLE IS present and undermining the structure of a church long before you see anything. The evidence of his burrowing is usually the first sign.

A church can appear to be totally healthy when observed with the natural eye, but it isn't long before a pastor becomes aware that something is wrong. He may not be able to put his finger on it, but he can sense something isn't right. It's like planting good seeds yet nothing sprouts up. After you plant three or four times and nothing ever grows, you soon stop planting seeds and start looking for the problem. It's time to find out what or who is devouring the seed.

It doesn't take a mental giant to know there's a mole in the church that devours every seed the church plants. Knowing a mole is present is the easy part. Knowing how to locate the mole is more difficult, and disposing of the mole is the final test.

I find three things hinder our ability to identify a mole.

Three Hindrances To Identifying A Mole

The first hindrance is our own intellect.

We look at a situation and logically sort through the facts and reach a conclusion.

In Isaiah 55:9 (NKJV) the Lord says, "My ways are higher than your ways,"

If we were able to use every brain cell we have in our heads and detail every fact at our grasp, we would still fall short of the true facts in many cases. Satan is the master counterfeiter. He comes as an angel of light and depends on deception to achieve his goals. Most often he makes the mole seem like the most loyal and spiritual member in the church.

A mole cannot operate without the confidence of the leadership. They must believe in the mole in order for him to be effective. If this is true, then the mole must appear to be one of the spiritual leaders of the church and one whose loyalty would never be questioned.

The second hindrance to identifying the mole is our emotions.

Remember the black ops units that instantly attack when they're discovered and then break off contact?

The same thing happens in the church world. The mole is well camouflaged and hidden so he won't be instantly seen. He does not appear to be a mole so we assume he isn't. It's not until we accidentally step on the mole that we are attacked.

The mole strikes suddenly and powerfully and then retreats back into his camouflaged identity. We, and many times our families, are left lying hurt and wounded on the roadside of ministry.

As a result of the attack we came face-to-face with the mole and identified him. We shared this new information with our council and they expressed their disbelief. The person that we accused could not possibly be the mole because he's been so faithful. We must be mistaken about what just happened.

Now, not only have we been injured emotionally, but no one believes what we are saying. It is about this time our emotions enter the picture. We've just been wounded and nobody believes our account. Disbelief and anger mix together to cloud our judgment and we are very close to making a mistake because of the hurts.

I know that pastors should have the fruit of the Spirit perfected in their lives and should never have outbursts of emotion, especially anger. But let's be honest. Pastors do let their emotions come to the surface and at times they do let their emotions affect their decisions. When this occurs, we pastors often make errors, especially when we deal with our families and churches.

The third hindrance to identifying the true mole is irritating personalities.

I don't know about you, but some personalities just irritate me. In the same sense, I know I irritate a lot of people. It's a simple fact of life. The problem is, we often let these little irritations cloud our judgment.

Sometimes we use the irritations as a symbol of the identification of the mole. It makes sense that the mole would have an irritating personality, but that's not necessarily the case. The mole is probably the most likeable person you will ever meet, but we often make judgments based on personal likes and dislikes.

We need to let God identify the mole. Through the leading of the Holy Spirit this can and will be done.

Three Steps to Identifying and Eliminating The Mole

There are three simple steps that can lead us to the identification and elimination of the mole. Not all moles need to be dealt with in the same manner, so the correct identification and elimination is extremely important.

Step One: Prayer

The first step sounds so simple that I almost did not include it in this chapter. I was thinking to myself that every pastor already knows prayer precedes all actions so it would be insulting to include such a basic step in this book.

After spending some time thinking and praying about it, I realized, while watching a boxing match, how we often make a mistake because we step away from the basics. The match I was watching pitted a boxer against a slugger. The difference between them is that the slugger will knock you out with one punch while the boxer will use a combination of many hits to win the match.

The boxer was doing very well by using the jab. Every time the slugger got close, the boxer would hit him. The slugger was unable to deliver a knockout punch because the jab the boxer was using kept him off balance.

During the fourth round, the slugger connected with a couple of hard hits that rocked the boxer. The boxer got mad and began to stray from the basics that had been winning the fight for him. He forgot his strategy and tried to slug it out with the slugger. Within two rounds, the boxer was knocked out. The boxer had been winning until he let his emotions interfere with his plan. Once his emotions interfered with his logic, he left the basics and lost the contest.

As ministers we know the importance of prayer. We know that without prayer we are fighting the battle on our own and inevitably we will lose. When the battle becomes personal, especially if it involves our family, our emotions often take over and cloud our judgment. If our family is being hurt, we enter a protective mode and often launch an impulsive defensive attack.

I know of one pastor who invited the offending church member to walk into the parking lot where they could settle the problem man-to-man. I am sure it was a spiritual endeavor because there were many references to the laying on of hands and many more references to the shedding of blood. (If you try to tell me that pastors never become angry or protective, then I can recite many more examples like this.)

I believe everyone knows the first victim of a personal battle is prayer. We forget Paul's writings to the Ephesians when he told them, "We wrestle not against flesh and blood, but against principalities and powers."

I don't believe Paul would have written this if he weren't dealing with a similar problem. The problem is basic to human nature. When the fight becomes personal, we tend to center on the individual rather than on principalities and powers. When this occurs, we usually stop praying and continue fighting. The assassin cannot get personally involved with his assignment. He must approach his assignment as strictly business and deal with it in a totally logical manner.

Another problem with prayer is that we often enter a defensive mode and are so busy putting up spiritual hedges around our families, our leadership, and our ministry that we forget to pray about the source of the problem. We tend to deal with the symptoms rather than the cause.

Prayer can and will reveal the root cause of the problem and can quickly lead us to the solution. The first step in rooting out the mole is to identify the real mole through a season of prayer.

Step Two: Love

The second step involves love. Again, this seems simple and something that shouldn't have to be addressed. In the real world, love also becomes the victim of a prolonged confrontation.

Jesus addressed this problem in Matthew 22:36-40 (NKJV):

> "Teacher, which is the great commandment in the law?"
>
> Jesus said to him, "You shall love the Lord your God with all your heart, with all your soul, and with all your mind. This is the first and great commandment. And the second is like it: You shall love your neighbor as yourself. On these two commandments hang all the Law and the Prophets."

This commandment to love is threefold, directing our love "upward" toward God, "inward" toward ourselves, and "outward" toward our fellow human beings.

Love can take many forms. It can be emotional as well as emotionless. Emotion does not control love. In fact, love controls emotion. I emphasize this fact because if a pastor deals with a problem without any emotion, he is often considered unfeeling and unloving. The simple fact is that he acts in a correct way more often if he can look at a problem objectively.

A jury is told to weigh the *evidence* not the *emotions* that violent crime stirs up. The jury needs to objectively judge the guilt or innocence of a defendant in a murder trial. Attorneys will often dismiss jurors who have been personally involved in a crime of violence. This is because they tend to make decisions based on emotions and psychological scars and not on evidence alone.

I would daresay the majority of pastors is unable to deal with a problem strictly on evidence, devoid of emotion, because of the love and sensitivity natural to pastors. Even if they were able to make a decision based totally on the evidence, they would have to deal with their emotions later.

I have talked with pastors who had to make tough decisions that hurt people and families. They took the corrective action, but they agonized over the resulting hurts for many years. There are also pastors who, because of their personalities, were able to make tough decisions, take corrective action, and never second-guess themselves or lose any sleep over the situation. They do the necessary job, and then let it go.

If assassins second guessed every situation they corrected, they would go insane or would hesitate the next time they were in a dangerous situation. Every police officer or Special Forces member knows that hesitation will kill. This is why they train every day, so their response becomes automatic. Whenever you begin to doubt your decisions, you need to change your specialty.

David allowed three problem areas to exist within his kingdom. These three areas began to weaken his kingdom and eventually endangered its very survival. I must assume David thought he was dealing with these men in love. The fact is, it wasn't love, it was only "sloppy *agape*" and it was endangering everyone else. In the same way, there are some pastors who operate in sloppy *agape* and think they are moving in love.

HOSPITAL OR REST HOME

I became the pastor of a small church that received many prophecies confirming it had a "hospital" anointing. The hospital anointing was defined as a church where hurting people could come for healing. At least, that's how the members of the church explained it to me.

There were many hurting people in the church. In fact, almost everyone there was a patient. I only found one or two doctors and there were others, who thought they were doctors but were obviously operating without a license or any training.

I immediately noticed the patients were all being given sloppy *agape*, but no one was really being healed by the Word of God. No one was taking responsibility for his or her sin. They were all placing the blame on Satan, society, upbringing, or anything else they could point their fingers at, but no one was taking responsibility. Rather than confront these people, the leadership "loved" them to death.

I eventually confronted the church leaders and told them that according to the prophecies, they were called to be a hospital not a rest home. A hospital is where you go for treatment. A rest home is a place where you lie around until you die.

The staff in a hospital loves and cares for the patient as much as the staff in a rest home, but each displays its love in a different manner based on expectations concerning the patient. In a hospital the patient undergoes treatment with an eye toward eventual healing and restoration. The treatment can be painful and the rehabilitation can be agonizing, but it is done in love.

When my dad went into the hospital for open heart surgery, the doctors performed the surgery and immediately began looking toward rehabilitation. Within a couple of days they insisted he get out of bed and start walking. At first I thought his nurse was a cold-blooded practitioner, who was devoid of any feelings. I even referred to her as "Attila the Hun." I found out later that she really cared for her patients and always did the best for them even if it caused her personal emotional pain. It hurt my dad to get out of bed and walk, but in the long run it was the best thing for him.

On the flip side of the coin, the staff in a rest home also loves and cares for its patients. The difference is that its job is to make the patients comfortable until they die. They don't expect their patients to recover.

The church I took over was a rest home not a hospital. The members were comfortable in their sin and with their wounds. No one was being healed. I informed the leadership and members that we were going to become the hospital God had called us to be and close down the rest home because it wasn't profitable. The patients now had to make a choice. They could either get out of bed and start the healing process of rehabilitation or they had a short time to find another rest home.

I believe many pastors are heading up a rest home in the mistaken belief that they operate a hospital. You can call a duck an eagle as much as you want, but if it quacks like a duck, then it is still a duck. You can call your church a hospital all you want but if everyone leaves the same way they came in, then your church is a rest home.

Paul deals with a similar situation in 1 Corinthians 5:1-5:

> It is actually reported that there is sexual immorality among you, and such sexual immorality as is not even named among the Gentiles – that a man has his father's wife! And you are puffed up, and have not rather mourned, that he who has done this deed might be taken away from among you. For I indeed, as absent in body but present in spirit, have already judged (as though I were present) him who has so done this deed. In the name of our Lord Jesus Christ, when you

are gathered together, along with my spirit, with
the power of our Lord Jesus Christ, deliver such
a one to Satan for the destruction of the flesh,
that his spirit may be saved in the day of the
Lord Jesus. (NKJV)

Paul went so far as to kick a man out of the
church because he was involved in immorality. This
man had every opportunity to repent and change
his ways but he refused. Paul had the man removed
from fellowship, not as punishment, but so that he
might be saved. Paul took this action to bring about
restoration.

Step Three: Intentional Action

There are two ways of dealing with entrenched
strongholds in a church. One is what I have already
referred to as the "Moses anointing."

Moses walked with the people for forty years
until at the end of forty years, all the stiff-necked
people were dead and the new generation could enter
the Promised Land. Moses did what God required
of him. God chose to let time eliminate the problem
and God said of Moses that he was faithful.

There are times when God requires a pastor to
walk lovingly with a stiff-necked people and let them
lie comfortably in their rest home until they slowly
pass away. The pastor who has the Moses anointing
will also have the temperament and personality to
fulfill that calling. I thank God for them, but I am
not one of them.

The second way to deal with the problem is the Benaiah anointing. Benaiah did in a couple of days what it took Moses forty years to accomplish. Benaiah was also called to perform the mission God had given him. He was perfectly suited for this specific mission and he eliminated the moles in quick order.

Moses was able to let time accomplish the job. He was able to relax and "go with the flow." Moses did not have to take intentional corrective action. He was able to love the people and encourage them as they died. Moses did not have to plan the takeover of the Promised Land, and he did not have to train the Israelites to be soldiers. All he had to do was make them comfortable.

Benaiah, on the other hand, had to know his opponents. The three men he was to assassinate did not want to die. It was obvious they would resist their untimely demise. Shimei was probably the least dangerous of the opponents. He was an older man with little or no military training. He was rash, spontaneous, and ruled by his emotions, especially anger. These weaknesses made him an easy target.

Adonijah was more dangerous than Shimei. He was young, plotting, deceptive, and would do anything to achieve his goal. His weakness was that he was a coward. When he was trying to take the throne from David, he was brave when he had support and seemed to be in power. When his supporters deserted him, he cried like a baby and pled for mercy. Without support, a coward will not fight when cornered.

Joab was the most dangerous of the three. He was a trained soldier and an expert on tactics. He had the ability to defend himself against well-trained opponents. He was also a brave man who, when cornered, would not surrender. He would face death bravely and end his life like a man.

A pastor called to the Benaiah anointing must take the time to identify the strengths and weaknesses of his opponents. When we know the identity of the mole within our church, we often rush to confrontation without doing our homework. Because we do not take action with intent, we underestimate our opponent. The opponent pulls a hidden weapon, and innocent church members become victims needlessly.

These bystanders might not have been injured if we had done our homework and planned accordingly. Collateral damage will often occur, but we can minimize it. Intentional action does not cause damage. It prevents it.

Identifying our opponents cannot be done by consulting with longtime members of the church. Many times the members we try talking to might just be the real moles. If the persons we consult with are moles, they will betray us and set a trap of their own.

A good assassin works alone. He observes his target, noting everything about him, even things that seem unimportant on the surface. The assassin will begin to identify patterns and through these patterns weaknesses will be identified. He will also identify personality types and when he fully knows his opponent, he will formulate a plan of action that will allow him to eliminate his target with the least collateral damage.

FINDING THE TRIGGER POINT

Every target has a weakness. Every man has a trigger that when pulled causes a reaction intended to eliminate the problem. In our haste to correct the problem, we don't usually take the time to locate the trigger.

I'm an avid chess player. I try to play one or two games every day. Chess is a battle between two opponents with the chessboard as the battleground and the pieces as our armies. There are many tactics and strategies that can be used to win the game. The strategy I use is based on my assessment of my opponent. I am not a great player but would probably be listed in the middle of the field. This example is given from that perspective.

I try to identify the style of play my opponent is most comfortable with. If he likes a slow strangulation type game where he protects every piece and hates to lose any men, I will quickly start capturing any man he leaves vulnerable and try to throw him off his game plan. I try to take him into an area he's not comfortable with. When I am playing medium- to lower-ranked players this is quite easy to do, but a great player will not submit to this tactic. If I am to beat a great player, I will have to use a totally different strategy. I will have to adapt my play to the quality of my opponent's if I am to win.

If we as pastors are to salvage a problem church, we have to be creative, adaptable, logical, and deliberate. The strongholds we identify in a man quite often hide or camouflage the very trigger we are searching for.

An example of this would be a man in your congregation who holds various titles within the church. He probably does a good enough job to be reappointed or reelected every year. If this person is the mole then he will protect his position and bring no suspicion on himself or his job. He will use his position to undermine other areas of the church, making it very difficult to identify himself or another as the mole. That is why surveillance is of utmost importance. You must locate the mole before you start pulling triggers.

One way to eliminate the type of a mole who covets titles is to find a way to remove the title as well as the prestige and authority that go with it. Many times this is the trigger that will cause this person to leave the church.

A friend of mine in a small city in California experienced this type of a problem. He had a man who was appointed as head usher. This man did a great job for a few years, then he began to undermine the pastor and the entire ministry. He would actually drive visitors away from the church by the way he treated them. To compound the problem, this man was related to 25 percent of the congregation. If he left, the other family members would also leave.

The pastor offered this man a new position that carried a bigger title and a bigger nametag. This was a new division within the church and the position would be for a term of one year. The man accepted the bigger title and assumed the new position. He no longer caused any problems as head usher. It was no surprise to anyone when the new position was eliminated at the end of the year.

The man was extremely angry when his position and title were not renewed and even angrier when he was not offered another title. He eventually left the church and the problem was truly eliminated. The point is that the pastor's plan worked. During the year this man held the new title, he was neutralized and when he left there was no fallout.

Some pastors would call this a game and say the pastor should have just confronted the man and openly removed him. But if the pastor had done that, many other people would have been hurt and the church would have suffered great loss.

This pastor took intentional, corrective action and eliminated the problem with the least collateral damage. The mole was identified and eliminated and the church was back on track.

CHAPTER 7

ESTABLISHING GOD'S KINGDOM

THE FACT THAT the church is at war is well documented in the Bible. 2 Corinthians 10:3-4 states:

> For though we walk in the flesh, we do not war after the flesh: (for the weapons of our warfare are not carnal, but mighty through God to the pulling down of strong holds; KJV).

There is a battle taking place in the invisible spiritual realm, but it is visible in the physical realm. One of the main places we see this battle is in our churches. The battle surfaces in our churches because they are the training grounds for the army of God. The fivefold ministry is involved in training the Army of God to do the work of the ministry (Eph. 4:11-13).

If Satan can stop the church from waging war, then he can defeat the soldiers one by one. Satan has launched an attack by infiltrating the churches and planting insurgents and moles within the leadership. The main targets of the resistance are the men and women who shepherd these churches. Our pastors lead the localized armies and are the ones who are best situated to wreak the most havoc on Satan and his forces.

Satan cannot win a prolonged battle with the army of God, so he resorts to guerilla tactics. The insurgents and moles are the hidden forces that have been planted in thriving vibrant churches and they attack with overwhelming force every time a pastor nears a spiritual breakthrough.

We have lost too many pastors to these attacks of Satan. Pastors have left the ministry believing they were failures because they could not bring growth to their assigned churches. They were not prepared nor expecting the type of church to which they were assigned. They were unaware that some churches must be cleaned of insurgents and moles before church growth can take place. They went in alone, like sheep to the slaughter unprepared for the lions' den that was waiting.

These pastors were not prepared spiritually or emotionally for the type of close combat they were about to be engaged in. There is a special type of pastor who, by his psychological makeup, is well-equipped for the type of battle required when fighting insurgents and moles. Church leaders need to identify these unique pastors and utilize them to clean out embedded insurgents and moles and prepare the church for the loving, longsuffering, church-growth focused pastors who should follow them.

Leadership needs to use a team effort to identify, root out, and eliminate the embedded opposition to the successful ministry God desires in His churches. We must take back our churches from the hands of Satan and establish them once again in the army of God.

After Solomon took advantage of the special gifting possessed by Benaiah, the assassin, 1 Kings 2:46 tells us:

> So the kingdom was established in Solomon's hand.

Some of our kingdoms (churches) need to be established and the sooner we bring that topic out of the closet and into the living room, the sooner the victory can be celebrated.

9 781414 113449